This Goal Planner Belongs To:

_____

Notes On Use

* It's widely known that "Failing to plan is like planning to fail." Use this planner to help you track your progress and achieve your goals.
* This planner allows you to track your goals for 12 months (with months listed, but undated). You can start the planner from whatever month you decide to achieve a goal and then continue for a year from then on. Or if you prefer a linear format, simply cross out the month names to start from whatever month you are starting the planner.
* Your plan doesn't have to be perfect! A bad plan is better then no plan, so just start and then adapt as you go.
* Perhaps write in pencil for the Main Action Plan and Future Years Goals Pages if you'd like to update these as you go.
* For each month there are Notes pages, Checklists, Monthly Progress Tracker Pages, Monthly Overview Pages and Vision Boards. These are to help you be specific and creative in envisioning and tracking your goals to reach success.
* Have Fun With it! You owe it to yourself to achieve what you want in life!

Goal Action Plan

Date

FOCUS

ACTION STEPS	DATE	✓	MILESTONES & REWARDS

Q1		Q2		Q3		Q4	
JAN		APR		JUL		OCT	
FEB		MAY		AUG		NOV	
MAR		JUN		SEP		DEC	

Future Goals

TIME FRAME	WHAT	ACTION PLAN
6 MONTHS		
1 YEAR		
3 YEARS		
5 YEARS		
10 YEARS		

Goals Checklist

FOR: DATE   ✓

This Year's Goals

GOAL	STEPS TO MAKE IT HAPPEN	DEADLINE	✓

GOAL	STEPS TO MAKE IT HAPPEN	DEADLINE	✓

GOAL	STEPS TO MAKE IT HAPPEN	DEADLINE	✓

Goals for...

DATE:

DATE:

DATE:

DATE:

DATE:

DATE:

January

Date: _____

_____

_____

_____

_____

_____

_____

_____

_____

_____

_____

_____

_____

_____

_____

_____

Vision Board

Goals Checklist

FOR: DATE ✓

Monthly Goal Progress

GOAL	GOAL

1	1
2	2
3	3
4	4
5	5
6	6
7	7
8	8
9	9
10	10
11	11
12	12

Monthly Overview

February

Date: _____

_____
_____
_____
_____
_____
_____
_____
_____
_____
_____
_____
_____
_____
_____
_____

Vision Board

Goals Checklist

FOR: DATE   ✓

Monthly Goal Progress

GOAL	GOAL

1	1
2	2
3	3
4	4
5	5
6	6
7	7
8	8
9	9
10	10
11	11
12	12

Monthly Overview

March

Date: _____

_____
_____
_____
_____
_____
_____
_____
_____
_____
_____
_____
_____
_____
_____
_____
_____

Vision Board

Goals Checklist

FOR: DATE   ✓

Monthly Goal Progress

GOAL	GOAL

1

1

2

2

3

3

4

4

5

5

6

6

7

7

8

8

9

9

10

10

11

11

12

12

Monthly Overview

April

Date: _____

_____

_____

_____

_____

_____

_____

_____

_____

_____

_____

_____

_____

_____

_____

Vision Board

Goals Checklist

FOR: DATE   ✓

Monthly Goal Progress

GOAL	GOAL

1	1
2	2
3	3
4	4
5	5
6	6
7	7
8	8
9	9
10	10
11	11
12	12

Monthly Overview

_____

_____

_____

_____

_____

_____

_____

_____

_____

_____

_____

May

Date: _____

_____
_____
_____
_____
_____
_____
_____
_____
_____
_____
_____
_____
_____
_____
_____

Vision Board

Goals Checklist

FOR: DATE ✓

Monthly Goal Progress

GOAL	GOAL

1	1
2	2
3	3
4	4
5	5
6	6
7	7
8	8
9	9
10	10
11	11
12	12

Monthly Overview

June

Date: _____

_____
_____
_____
_____
_____
_____
_____
_____
_____
_____
_____
_____
_____
_____
_____
_____
_____
_____

Vision Board

Goals Checklist

FOR: DATE ✓

Monthly Goal Progress

GOAL	GOAL

1	1
2	2
3	3
4	4
5	5
6	6
7	7
8	8
9	9
10	10
11	11
12	12

Monthly Overview

July

Date: _____

Vision Board

Goals Checklist

FOR: DATE ✓

Monthly Goal Progress

GOAL	GOAL

1	1
2	2
3	3
4	4
5	5
6	6
7	7
8	8
9	9
10	10
11	11
12	12

Monthly Overview

August

Date: _____

Vision Board

Goals Checklist

FOR: DATE   ✓

Monthly Goal Progress

GOAL	GOAL

1	1
2	2
3	3
4	4
5	5
6	6
7	7
8	8
9	9
10	10
11	11
12	12

Monthly Overview

September

Date: _____

Vision Board

Goals Checklist

FOR: DATE ✓

Monthly Goal Progress

GOAL	GOAL

1	1
2	2
3	3
4	4
5	5
6	6
7	7
8	8
9	9
10	10
11	11
12	12

Monthly Overview

October

Date: _____

Vision Board

Goals Checklist

FOR: DATE ✓

Monthly Goal Progress

GOAL	GOAL

1	1
2	2
3	3
4	4
5	5
6	6
7	7
8	8
9	9
10	10
11	11
12	12

Monthly Overview

November

Date: _____

_____

_____

_____

_____

_____

_____

_____

_____

_____

_____

_____

_____

_____

_____

Vision Board

Goals Checklist

FOR: DATE   ✓

Monthly Goal Progress

GOAL	GOAL

1

1

2

2

3

3

4

4

5

5

6

6

7

7

8

8

9

9

10

10

11

11

12

12

Monthly Overview

_____

_____

_____

_____

_____

_____

_____

_____

_____

_____

December

Date: _____

_____

_____

_____

_____

_____

_____

_____

_____

_____

_____

_____

_____

_____

_____

_____

Vision Board

Goals Checklist

FOR: DATE   ✓

Monthly Goal Progress

GOAL	GOAL

1	1
2	2
3	3
4	4
5	5
6	6
7	7
8	8
9	9
10	10
11	11
12	12

Monthly Overview

Printed in Great Britain
by Amazon

22324791R00057